Why the Dinosaurs Died Out

Sally Cowan

Why the Dinosaurs Died Out

Text: Sally Cowan
Publishers: Tania Mazzeo and Eliza Webb
Series consultant: Amanda Sutera
  Hands on Heads Consulting
Editor: Laken Ballinger
Project editor: Annabel Smith
Designer: Leigh Ashforth
Project designer: Danielle Maccarone
Illustrations: Mat Edwards
Maps: Wayne Murphy
Permissions researchers: Corrina and Marlo Gilbert
Production controller: Renee Tome

Acknowledgements
We would like to thank the following for permission to reproduce
copyright material:

p. 6: Alamy Stock Photo/Phil Degginger; p. 9 (top): Lawrence Berkeley
Laboratory, cc-by-sa 4.0, https://creativecommons.org/licenses/by-sa/4.0/,
(bottom): D. VAN RAVENSWAAY/SCIENCE PHOTO LIBRARY;
p. 18: Shutterstock.com/Ammit Jack; p. 19: ©2018 Planet Labs, Inc. cc-by-
sa 4.0, https://creativecommons.org/licenses/by-sa/4.0/;
p. 22 (left): Alamy Stock Photo/Buddy Mays, (right): BRITISH ANTARCTIC
SURVEY/SCIENCE PHOTO LIBRARY; p. 23 (top): Alamy Stock Photo/dpa
picture alliance, (bottom): PASCAL GOETGHELUCK/SCIENCE PHOTO
LIBRARY.

Every effort has been made to trace and acknowledge copyright.
However, if any infringement has occurred, the publishers tender their
apologies and invite the copyright holders to contact them.

NovaStar
Reading age: 8–8.5

Cengage Learning Australia
Level 5, 80 Dorcas Street
Southbank VIC 3006 Australia
Phone: 1300 790 853
Email: aust.nelsonprimary@cengage.com

For learning solutions, visit cengage.com.au

Printed in China by 1010 Printing International Ltd
1 2 3 4 5 6 7 28 27 26 25 24

*Nelson acknowledges the Traditional Owners and Custodians
of the lands of all First Nations Peoples. We pay respect
to Elders past and present, and extend that respect to
all First Nations Peoples today.*

Contents

Different Ideas

Over 200 million years ago, the first dinosaurs appeared in the world. For the next 165 million years, an amazing variety of dinosaurs roamed Earth. There were small, chicken-sized dinosaurs, fierce meat-eating giants, and huge plant-eaters, which were the largest creatures that ever lived on land.

But 66 million years ago, the dinosaurs died out. Scientists have different ideas about why this happened.

Timeline of When the Dinosaurs Lived

The time when the dinosaurs lived is divided into three periods, or parts: the Triassic, Jurassic and Cretaceous periods.

250–200 MA

Triassic Period
The first dinosaurs appear around 230 MA.

200–145 MA

Jurassic Period

MA = million years ago

The *Procompsognathus*, which was about the size of a chicken, lived during the Triassic Period.

The *Brachiosaurus* lived during the Jurassic Period and was one of the largest dinosaurs.

The *Spinosaurus* from the Cretaceous Period was the largest meat-eating dinosaur.

145–66 MA

Cretaceous Period

66 MA

The dinosaurs died out.

Many scientists believe it was an **asteroid** that hit Earth and suddenly killed all the dinosaurs. Some scientists believe that the dinosaurs died out slowly over a few million years due to shifting land and a colder **climate**. And other scientists believe that erupting volcanoes poisoned the dinosaurs' **habitat**.

From Dinosaurs to Birds

Some small dinosaurs slowly changed into birds over time. Birds did not die out like the dinosaurs.

The **evidence** for these ideas can be found in layers of rock on Earth. Scientists study rock around dinosaur fossils to learn what was happening on Earth at that time.

Scientists study the rock around fossils to look for evidence of changes to the land.

Some scientists believe the dinosaurs were killed by an asteroid hitting Earth.

Some scientists believe dinosaurs could have died out because of erupting volcanoes.

A Gigantic Asteroid

Many scientists believe that a gigantic asteroid hit Earth 66 million years ago. They say that the **impact** caused several natural disasters that the dinosaurs could not survive.

The asteroid that hit Earth 66 million years ago was several kilometres wide.

In the early 1980s, when scientists Luis and Walter Alvarez noticed a rare metal in rock found from that time period, they thought the metal might have come from an exploding asteroid. This metal is called "iridium". Also, a large **crater** was discovered off the coast of Mexico in 1978, making the asteroid idea more popular.

Father and son Luis and Walter Alvarez helped come up with the asteroid idea.

The Chicxulub Crater

The crater off the coast of Mexico is called the Chicxulub (say: *chick–zu–loob*) crater. Many scientists think it is the right size and shape for the gigantic asteroid impact.

This image shows the area where scientists found the Chicxulub crater off the coast of Mexico.

A Sudden End

When the asteroid crashed into Earth, it caused a powerful explosion that blasted the asteroid into pieces. Dust, ash and tiny bits of burning rock shot up into the **atmosphere**.

A huge shock wave of heat from the explosion went out across the land and sea. It burned everything in its path. The dinosaurs caught in the shock wave died instantly.

Bits of burning rock from the explosion fell on the dinosaurs that survived the shock wave.

Tsunamis crashed onto the land and swept away the dinosaurs that were too close.

When burning bits of rock from the explosion fell back to Earth, they started fires all over the planet. The fires burned most of the world's forests.

The asteroid impact also caused massive earthquakes and **tsunamis**. Water flooded large areas of land, drowning the dinosaurs that lived there.

Dust blocked sunlight for years, which made Earth colder. The dinosaurs were used to living in a warmer climate, so they could not survive the sudden cold weather.

Also, the dinosaurs' **food chain** had been ruined. The plants were poisoned by **acid rain** and could not grow without enough sunlight. The plant-eating dinosaurs soon starved. In turn, the meat-eating dinosaurs starved, because there were not enough plant-eating dinosaurs for them to eat.

Earth was too cold and empty for the dinosaurs to survive after the asteroid impact.

Evidence for the asteroid idea

➡️ The metal iridium was found in a layer of rock from 66 million years ago. Iridium is found in asteroids.

➡️ The huge Chicxulub crater was discovered off the coast of Mexico.

➡️ A layer of burnt vegetation and possible rubble from a tsunami was found in some rock layers from this time.

Shifting Land and a Colder Climate

Scientists tested rock from long ago to find out about the climate at the time. They discovered that shifting land made the climate colder during the last 10 million years that the dinosaurs lived. The colder climate made it much harder for the dinosaurs to survive. Some scientists believe this is why the dinosaurs died out.

Slow Changes

In the time of the dinosaurs, the land on Earth was very different to what it is today. There was one large **land mass** called Pangaea (say: *pan-jee-a*). It slowly split apart over millions of years.

A Supercontinent

Pangaea was a supercontinent.
This means that all the continents in the world today were once joined together in this supercontinent.

As the land broke into pieces, it became surrounded by water. The wind from the seas then cooled the land. Some dinosaurs died out because they could not **adapt** to the lower temperature, which had dropped by about 8 degrees Celsius.

PANGAEA
225 MILLION YEARS AGO

THE CONTINENTS
TODAY

Scientists think the continents fitted together like puzzle pieces to make Pangaea before they split apart into the continents we have today.

The colder climate killed off some of the plants that the dinosaurs ate. New flowering plants grew instead. Many of the plant-eating dinosaurs died because they could not adapt to eating the flowering plants. That meant there was less meat for the meat-eating dinosaurs, so some of them died out, too.

But scientists believe some types of dinosaurs were able to adapt to live in the colder climate. So the change in climate might not fully explain why all the dinosaurs died out.

Evidence for the colder climate idea

- The land mass Pangaea broke up into smaller continents.

- Scientists can test rock to find out what the climate was like when the rock was formed.

- Rubble in the rock may be due to changes in sea levels, rather than a tsunami.

- Fewer types of dinosaur fossils have been found in the rock from the late Cretaceous Period.

Some dinosaurs may have been able to survive in the colder climate after the land shifted.

Volcanoes

Scientists have a third idea about why the dinosaurs died out. They have found evidence of enormous volcanic eruptions that happened in India around 66 million years ago, in a place called the Deccan Traps. These eruptions could have wiped out the dinosaurs.

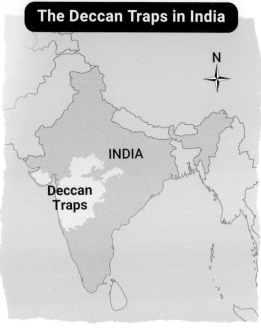

The Deccan Traps in India

N

INDIA

Deccan Traps

Lots of erupting volcanoes could have caused the dinosaurs to die out.

The Deccan Traps in India have layers in the rock that formed from volcanic eruptions.

Importantly, scientists have discovered that iridium, the metal found in asteroids, is also found deep inside Earth. This iridium is released into the atmosphere when volcanoes erupt. That could be why iridium was found in the layer of rock from 66 million years ago.

The Deccan Traps

The Deccan Traps are rock formations of ancient lava flows that cover a large part of India. The word "traps" is used to describe rock that looks like a set of steps.

Habitat Destroyed

The volcanic eruptions released gases and clouds of ash and dust, which slowly spread around Earth. The climate became hotter, and the air was poisonous to breathe. Acid rain polluted the land and oceans.

Just like with the asteroid, the dinosaurs' habitat burned, and their food chains were ruined. The eruptions went on for such a long time that there was no chance of the dinosaurs surviving.

Evidence for the volcanoes idea

➡ The Deccan Traps in India have areas of thick rock 2 kilometres deep, formed by enormous ancient lava flows. The rock has been dated from around 67–66 million years ago.

➡ Iridium is released from deep inside Earth during volcanic eruptions. The metal iridium was found in the layer of rock from 66 million years ago.

➡ A layer of burnt vegetation was found in some rock layers from that time.

Acid rain from the volcanoes destroyed the dinosaurs' food chains.

An Exciting Puzzle

No one can know for sure why the dinosaurs died out because it happened so long ago. But scientists can try to fit the evidence together, like working on a jigsaw puzzle with many pieces.

Was it a sudden event or slow changes that killed off the dinosaurs? Scientists hope to make more exciting discoveries and get closer to the answer.

Scientists continue to study rock layers for clues about the dinosaurs.

As more dinosaur fossils are found, scientists can make more discoveries.

Scientists study dinosaur bones in a museum to learn more about how they died.

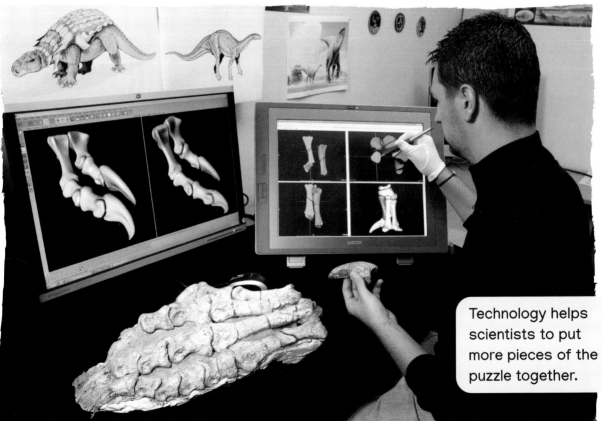

Technology helps scientists to put more pieces of the puzzle together.

Glossary

acid rain (*noun*)	rain that has taken in dangerous pollution from the air
adapt (*verb*)	become used to something, such as weather patterns
asteroid (*noun*)	a very large piece of rock that orbits the Sun
atmosphere (*noun*)	the layer of gases around Earth, including air
climate (*noun*)	the weather patterns throughout the year
crater (*noun*)	a bowl-shaped hole in the ground made when something hits with force
evidence (*noun*)	proof that something happened
food chain (*noun*)	a group of plants and animals that depend on each other as a source of food
habitat (*noun*)	a place where animals usually live
impact (*noun*)	when objects hit or crash into each other
land mass (*noun*)	a large unbroken area of land
tsunamis (*noun*)	extremely large waves caused by earthquakes or explosions

Index